LEARNING WORKS PARENTS & PRESCHOOLERS SERIES

WATER WIZARD

WRITTEN BY EDITH H. FINE & JUDITH P. JOSEPHSON

ILLUSTRATED BY BEV ARMSTRONG

Contents

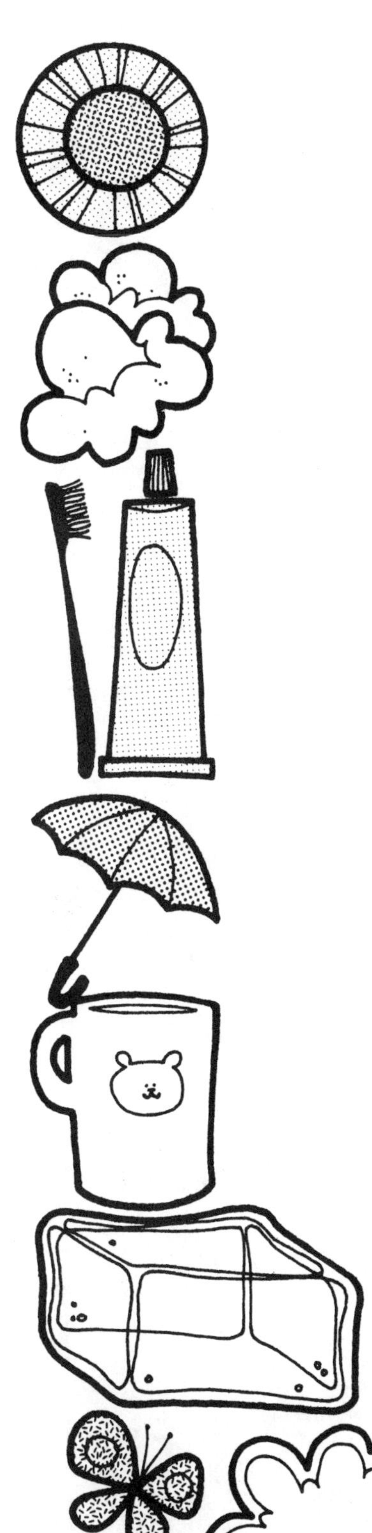

A Note to Parents

Water Wizard is for parents and young children to enjoy together. Water, wet and wonderful, is a daily part of children's first learning experiences—a friendly and a fascinating partner in early play.

Preschoolers are naturally drawn to water. They race through sprinklers on the lawn and wade in the waves at the shore. As they splash and spray, pour and fill, they intuitively absorb information about volume, gravity, density, and about how water behaves.

Water Wizard is divided into two sections. The pages in the first section are for parents to read aloud to children. On these pages you will find information about water and about specific ways in which you can explore water with your child. The Going Further pages offer additional activities and include titles of excellent books about water. Choose those activities and resources that are appropriate for your child, then dive in with ideas of your own.

The second section, entitled Water Wonder, consists of activity pages to strengthen specific readiness skills. Adapt them to your child's needs and interests. Use both sections of this book to make learning about water a joyful, splashy, giggly experience. Jump in — the water's fine!

Water Every Day

We use water every day for little jobs and big jobs. With water we brush our teeth, sprinkle the lawn, and take a shower or bath. We also wash our dishes and our clothes. We cook noodles, oatmeal, and eggs in water. Sometimes water heats or cools the air.

How does water reach our homes? Water comes from far away. It travels through pipes under streets and sidewalks. Pipes inside walls bring water to our tubs, sinks, and washing machines. Different pipes carry away the used or dirty water.

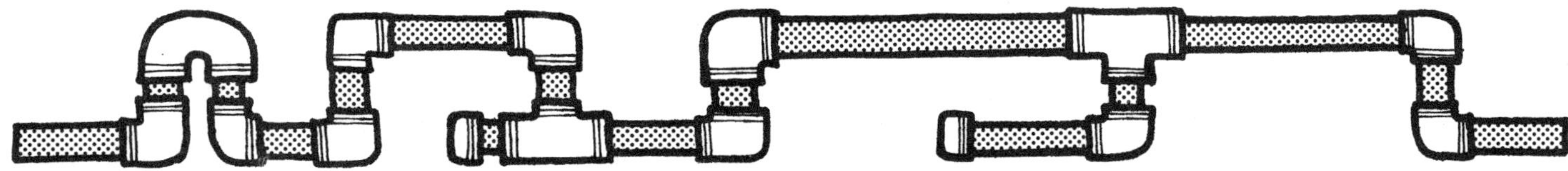

Be Water Wizards

- Some of the best birthday gifts can come from hardware and home supply stores. Plastic PVC pipe in various lengths with plenty of connectors is wonderful for building free-form structures. Gaskets for hoses and faucets can be threaded onto clothesline for small muscle practice. A rotating sprinkler for the hose is worth ten battery-operated toys. Small sections of pipe, a real wrench, washers, and other fascinating gadgets make a "plumber's kit."
- Have wet races with drops of liquids on a cookie sheet. Put one drop of water, one drop of milk, and one drop of oil at one end of a cookie sheet. Guess which drop will reach the other end first. Tip the tray up to start the race. Which drop won? Why? Try other liquids.
- Adult's work is child's play. Include your child in a variety of wet household chores, from doing dishes to scrubbing tubs and mopping up spills.
- Use a paintbrush and a bucket of water to practice writing letters and numbers on the sidewalk.

Do Water Wonder page 13, How Do We Use Water?

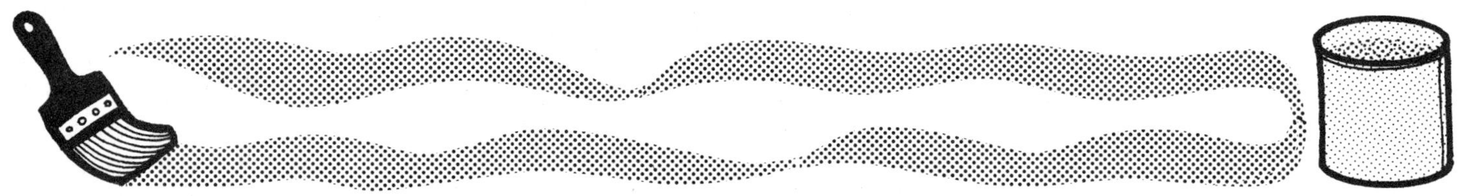

Water at Work

Water works hard in the world and helps us wherever we are—at home or at school, in cities or on farms, in factories or in offices, at work or at play. All living things need water—children and grown-ups, dogs and cats, polar bears and penguins, flowers and trees.

Although plants, animals, and people look very different, they all are made mostly of water. The water doesn't just slosh and bubble around inside them. In plants, leaves and stems hold water. In animals and people, water is part of the blood, bones, muscles, and other tissues.

It's funny, but plants, animals, and people are mostly water.

Be Water Wizards

- Put water to work on a hot summer day by using hoses and sprinklers to cool off small bodies.
- Use an outgrown baby bathtub for water play. Supply plenty of water toys and measuring tools, such as plastic cups, spoons, turkey basters, straws, sponges, and sieves.
- While at the beach or in the bath, bring informal number talk to water play. You can say things like, *I see **two** tiny toes. You found **three** beautiful shells. It takes **three** red cups of water* (or *sand) to fill this big blue one.*

Do Water Wonder page 24, Watch Me Grow.

Water All Around

Did you know that there is more water on our big earth than there is land? Look at a globe or map of the world and see how much more blue there is than other colors. We find water in puddles and ponds, lakes and reservoirs, streams and rivers, seas and oceans.

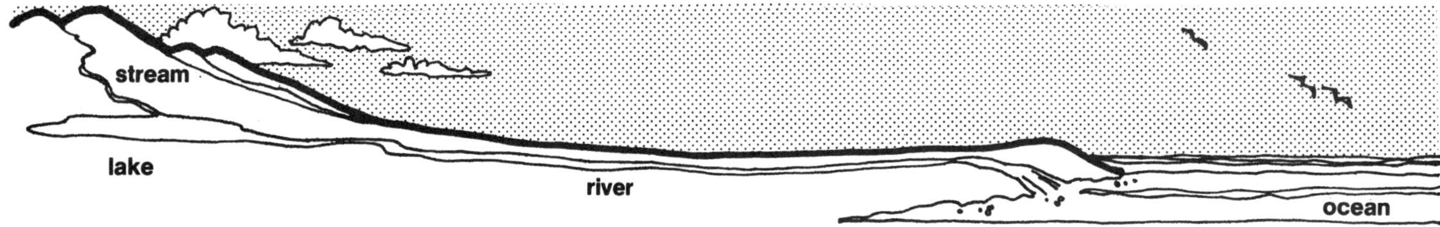

Water is always moving from place to place. A rushing river begins high in the mountains as a tiny stream. As it tumbles down the mountain, other streams flow into it, and it grows bigger and stronger. Down mountainsides and through valleys, rivers carry water to the oceans.

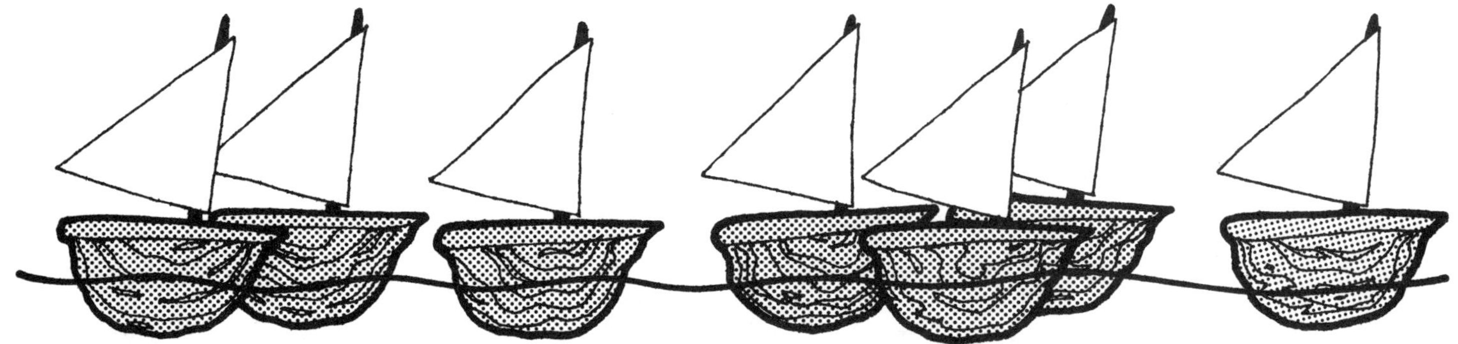

Be Water Wizards

- Find and observe different bodies of water, from puddles of rainwater to quiet ponds, larger lakes, gurgling streams, and rushing rivers.
- Visit a place where water is helping people—a dam, a harbor, or a laundromat.
- Read A. A. Milne's story "In Which Pooh Invents a New Game and Eeyore Joins In" on pages 235-250 in *The World of Pooh: The Complete Winnie-the-Pooh and The House at Pooh Corner* (New York: E. P. Dutton, 1957). Play the game with leaves, sticks, or tiny walnut shell boats. A downhill gutter works almost as well as Pooh's bridge.

Do Water Wonder page 23, Little Boats to Mighty Ships.

When Water Is Home

Many, many plants and animals live in and around water. Some of them prefer the salty water of the seas and oceans. Others choose the fresh water of ponds and lakes.

Ocean plants can be small or large. Some of them are so small that you would need a magnifying glass or a microscope to see them. Others are very large. One kind of seaweed, called a giant kelp, grows to be 100 feet long.

Ocean animals can also be small or large. At the ocean's edge, in the tiny, wet world of the tide pools, live many little creatures—crabs, sea anemones, and sea urchins. Many of them are so small you could easily hold one in your hand. Out in the ocean swims the blue whale. This animal grows to be 100 feet long—as long as a jet airplane—and is one of the biggest creatures that has ever lived on the earth.

Beavers, cranes, ducks, fish, frogs, and turtles make their homes in fresh water. They live among the cattails, reeds, and lily pads of ponds, lakes, creeks, and streams.

People often live close to water. Long ago, before pipes brought water to homes, people built their houses near the water. They needed it to drink, to cook and wash with, and to grow their food. They used it to ship the food they grew and the things they made to other towns and cities.

People often live near water. They fish in water, and use it to ship logs, grain, and coal to other places. For fun, children swim in water.

Be Water Wizards

- Goldfish and snails make nice water pets for preschoolers. With their noses pressed to the sides of a fishbowl or aquarium, they can observe how fish breathe and swim.
- Read about or visit ocean tide pools. Marvel at these tiny mini-worlds, but don't disturb the residents!
- In a pond or creek, find polliwogs, or tadpoles, to put in a jar and watch at home. Use the water you find them in, and feed them goldfish food. Notice the changes that take place as they grow into toads or frogs.

Do Water Wonder pages 17, Who Lives in Water? and 19, Fish Fun.

Water in the Weather

Every day, weather is part of what we do. We wake up when the sun peeks through the curtains, shut our windows during a thunderstorm, and check the weather when planning a picnic or parade.

Water is part of weather. **Weather** is how hot or cold, still or windy, and dry or wet the air is. Water in weather is magic! Right before our eyes, it can be a **gas**, a **liquid**, or a **solid.**

As fog or steam, water is a **gas.** When the weather is **foggy**, tiny droplets of water hang in the air. **Steam** rises from a pot of boiling water on the stove.

Liquid water is all around us. We turn on the faucet for a bath, and water runs out. When it rains, drops of water fall on our faces. **Rain** makes puddles on sidewalks and turns dirt into mud.

When the air is very cold, water freezes into **ice**, or **solid water. Snow** is tiny ice crystals. **Sleet** is frozen raindrops. **Hail** is larger balls of ice. These ice balls are called hailstones. They can be smaller than marbles or larger than golfballs.

Be Water Wizards

- Use an outside thermometer to measure the temperature in sunlight and shade, in summer and winter, and at dawn, noon, and dusk.
- Hang two wet cloths to dry, one in sunlight and one in shade. Which cloth dries first? Why?
- Put a widemouthed jar with straight, vertical sides out in a rain shower. As you do so ask, *Do you think we'll catch some rain?* After the shower, measure your "catch" in inches.
- Take rainy day walks together. Talk about what you see and feel.
- Draw pictures of rain and make up poems to go with them.
- Cut simple paper snowflakes. Fold a square of paper into quarters. Make tiny snips along the folded edges with scissors. Unfold and enjoy.
- Let real snow fall on a sheet of black construction paper. Look at the individual snowflakes. Then use a magnifying glass so you can get a closer look at the crystals.

Do Water Wonder pages 14, Make a Rainy Day, and 18, Writing Weather Words.

Going Further

For water wizards, here are some additional activity and resource ideas.

Mixtures and Magic

- Place a glass upside down on the lawn. Watch moisture from the ground gradually collect inside.
- Mix salt into water and drop or pour small amounts of this mixture on two shallow saucers. Place one saucer in the shade and one saucer in the sun. Check the saucers later the same day and again several days later. What happens? What's left?
- Put hot water in one bowl and cold water in another bowl. Drop an ice cube into each bowl. Which ice cube melts and vanishes first? Why?
- Try some kitchen chemistry. On a cookie sheet, place a muffin tin and six paper cups. Fill three of the paper cups with liquids—vinegar, oil, and water colored with food coloring. Fill the other three cups with solids—flour, salt, and baking soda. Encourage your child to combine small amounts of one liquid and one solid in each muffin tin cup. Mix and stir to make fizzy potions. (**Note:** Caution your child *never* to taste any unknown mixture without permission.)
- Explore with drops of water. Put a sheet of wax paper over the comic section of the Sunday paper. With an eyedropper, squeeze drops of water on to the wax paper. See how the drops magnify the letters. Ask questions such as, *What's the tiniest drop you can make? The biggest?*
- Young scientists love to work with water. Try sink-or-float experiments with everyday household items such as carrots, corks, erasers, nails, nuts, paper clips, peppercorns, plastic and wooden spools, spoons, and sponges.

Do Water Wonder page 20, Sink or Float?

Going Further
(continued)

Watery Fun

- Lemonade and popcorn are water-filled treats. Lemonade is mostly water. Popcorn kernels contain moisture, too. When these kernels are heated in the popper, the water in them expands and causes them to explode into puffs of popped corn.
- Weather words intrigue young children. Choose playful adjectives such as *misty-moisty, sizzling,* and *supercalifragilisticexpialidocious* to describe the day.
- Children enjoy dressing for the weather. A. A. Milne's poem "Happiness" describes a child's joy at having new rain apparel. Find the poem in *The World of Christopher Robin* (New York: E. P. Dutton, 1958) or in *When We Were Very Young* (New York: E. P. Dutton, 1924).
- A boat collection provides hours of water play in the bathtub, in puddles, and in ponds. Share with your child the poem "Where Go the Boats?" in *A Child's Garden of Verses* by Robert Louis Stevenson. No fewer than ten editions of this book are in print, including one especially for preschoolers published by Platt & Munk in 1980.
- For outdoor fun, mix liquid dishwashing detergent with water. Blow bubbles through many kinds of frames, bubble pipes, and wands. Shape bubbles with an eyedropper, funnel, or plastic turkey baster. Watch where they go. Before they float away, find the rainbow in each one.

Resources

Keats, Ezra Jack. *The Snowy Day.* New York: Viking, 1962.
Lionni, Leo. *Swimmy.* New York: Random House–Pantheon Books, 1963.
Macaulay, David. *Underground.* Boston: Houghton Mifflin, 1976.
McCloskey, Robert. *Make Way for Ducklings.* New York: Penguin, 1976.
McKie, Roy, and Philip D. Eastman. *Snow.* New York: Random House–Beginner, 1962.
Spier, Peter. *The Erie Canal.* Garden City, N.Y.: Doubleday, 1970.
_____. *London Bridge Is Falling Down.* Garden City, N.Y.: Doubleday, 1967.
Tresselt, Alvin. *Hide and Seek Fog.* New York: Lothrop, Lee & Shepard, 1965.
_____. *Rain Drop Splash.* New York: Lothrop, Lee & Shepard, 1946.

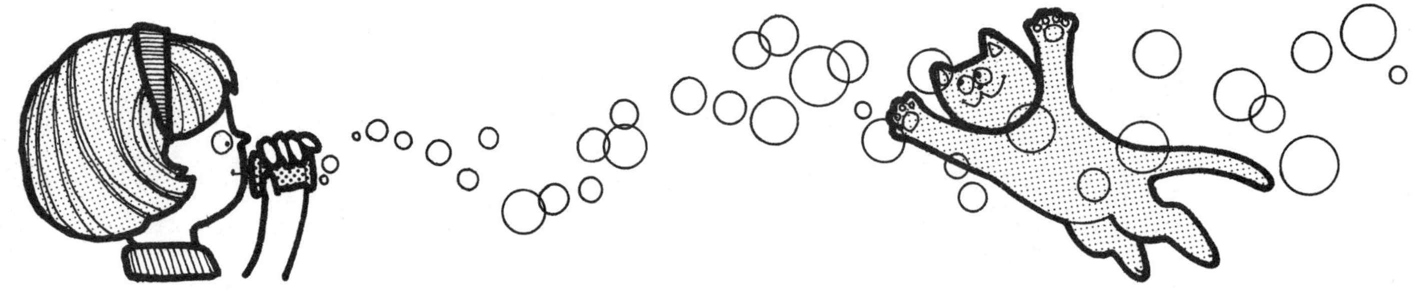

WATER WONDER BOOK

Note to Parents: The Water Wonder pages that follow are for your child. You can keep this section intact or remove these pages to make a separate book. Either way, encourage your child to color this cover. Write your child's name and the date on the lines below. Have your child select and glue a snapshot from a recent water adventure in this frame. Invent your own Water Wonder pages and add them, along with your child's favorite photographs and drawings, to the book.

by

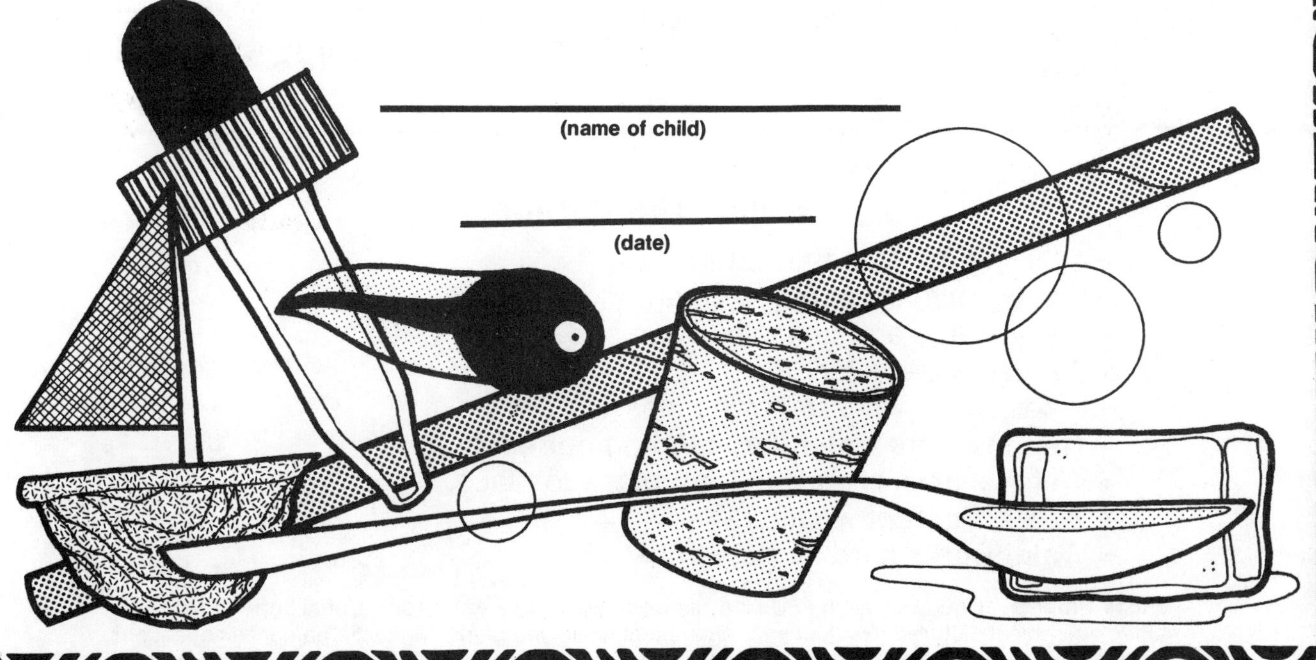

Skills: Vocabulary Development
Reading Readiness
Nurturing Curiosity
Memory

Water Words

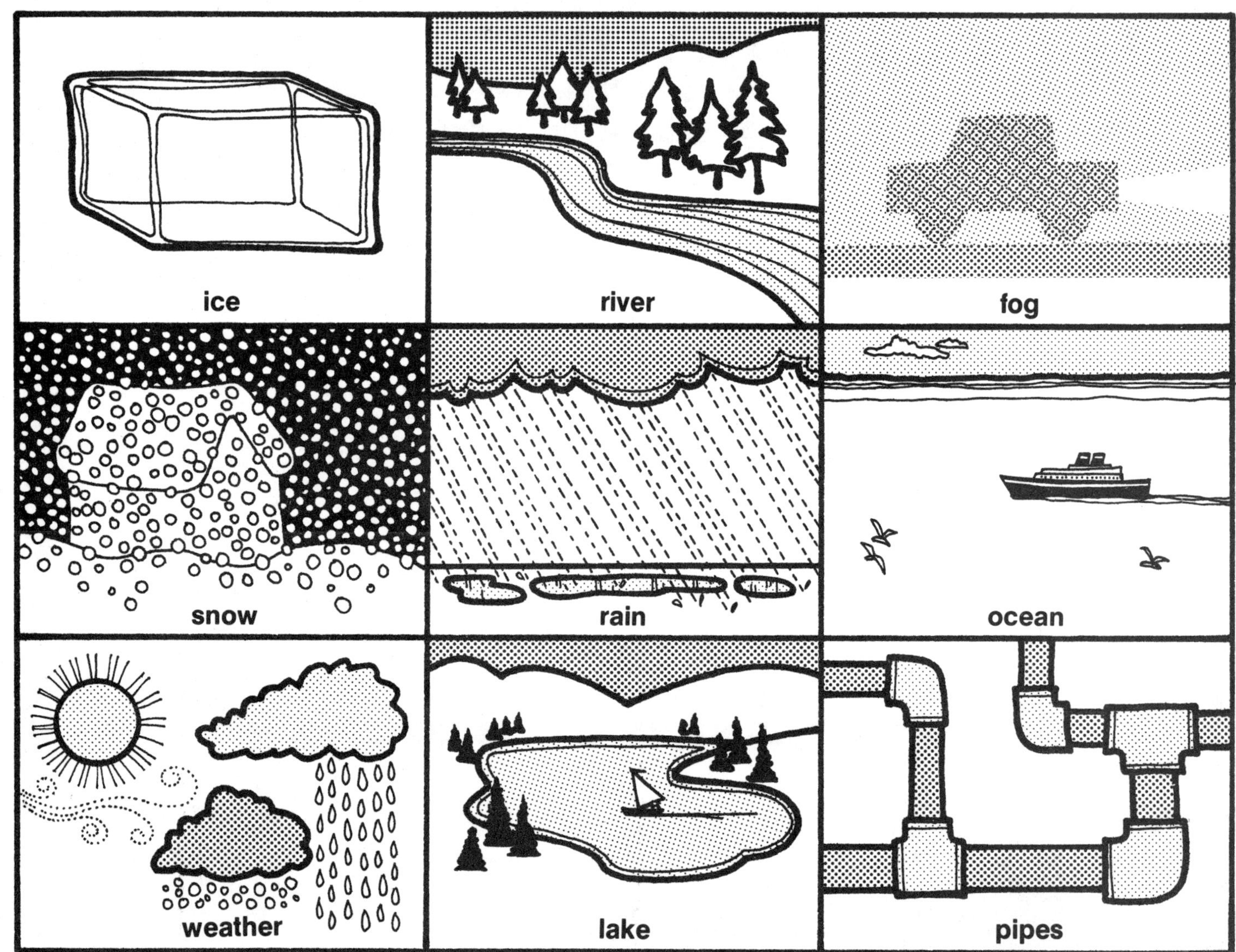

Water: The Big Idea

- All living things need water.
- Plants, animals, and people are mostly water.
- Many plants and animals live in and around water.
- We use water every day.
- Pipes carry water to our houses.
- There is more water than land on our earth.
- Water is always moving from place to place.
- Water is part of weather.
- Water works hard in the world.

Note to Parents: One at a time, point to the pictures on this page. As you do so, challenge your child to name each object pictured. Then let your child point while you name. Make it a game. Ask questions that relate these words to your child's own environment and experiences: *Where can you see **pipes** in our house? What kind of **weather** do we have today? What do you wear when it **snows**?*

Skills: Reasoning
Seeing Relationships

How Do We Use Water?

Draw a line from the water to the person who uses it.

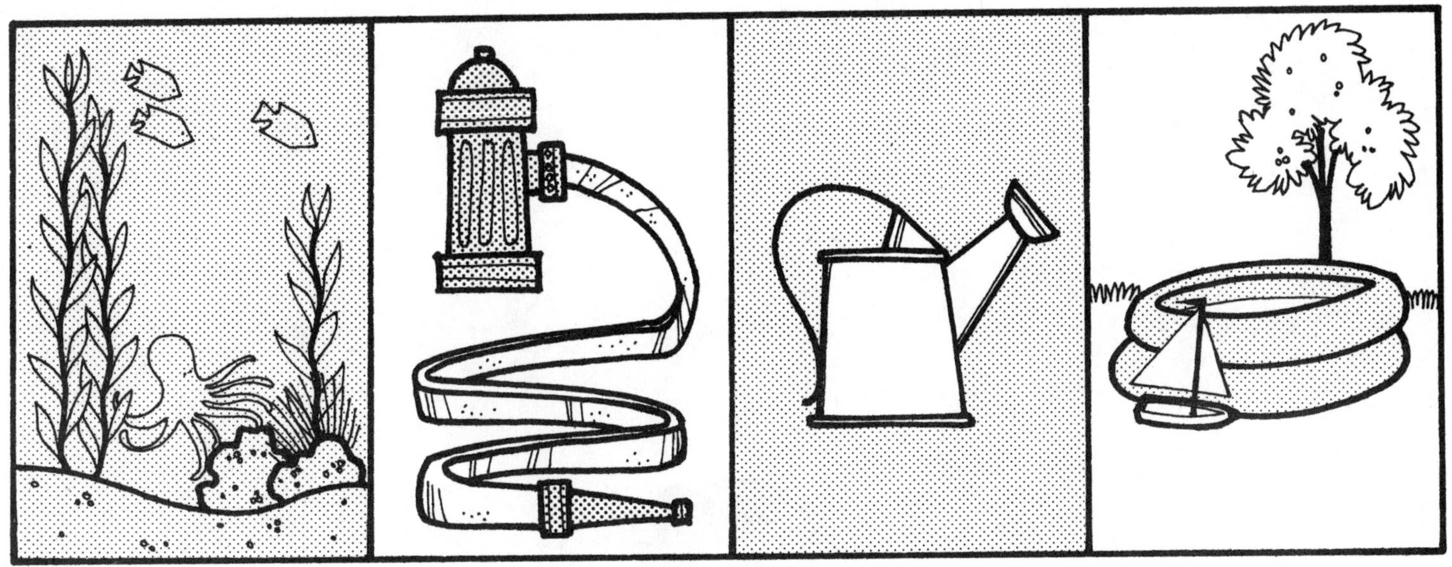

Note to Parents: Help your child see how many ways we use water. Talk about these pictures. Then read the instructions aloud. Ask, *Who will use the watering can? Who is dressed for pool play?* (See page 5, Water at Work.)

Skills: Eye-Hand Coordination
Figure-Ground Discrimination
Visual Memory

Make a Rainy Day

Follow the dotted lines to make clouds, an umbrella, and a puddle. Add raindrops, and you have a rainy day.

Note to Parents: Talk with your child about changes in the weather. Ask, *What does it take to turn a sunny day into a rainy one?* Provide crayons or chalk for coloring this picture. Have your child draw along the dotted lines to make clouds, an umbrella, and a puddle. Your child can also add raindrops by dotting the page with blue or gray. (See page 8, Water in the Weather.)

Skills: Reasoning
Observation
Visual Memory

Can This Hold Water?

Draw a circle around the things that can hold water.

Note to Parents: One at a time, point to the pictures on this page and name the objects. As you do so, encourage your child to guess which ones will hold water. Then gather objects similar to the ones pictured and test these guesses. Some of the objects, such as the hat and envelope, may hold water for a short time, but not for long!

Skills: Seeing Relationships
Logical Thinking

A Mixed-up Water World

Tell what's wrong in this mixed-up water world. Then color the picture.

Note to Parents: Here's a page to stretch language and thinking skills. Before your child colors it ask, *Which way is the rain going? What's silly about that boy? Why wouldn't that umbrella work? How could you change this picture to make it right? What other funny things could you add?*

Skills: Memory
Logical Thinking
Associating Ideas

Who Lives in Water?

Circle the animals that live in water. Then color the pictures.

Note to Parents: Talk about where these animals live. Ask, *Could a kitty live in the tide pools? Does this starfish live in a doghouse? Could Mrs. Whale come over to play at our house? Does Mr. Elephant get his peanuts in a pond?* (See page 7, When Water Is Home.)

Skills: Fine Motor Skills
Reading Readiness
Printing

Writing Weather Words

Follow the arrows to make real words. The pictures show you what words you are writing.

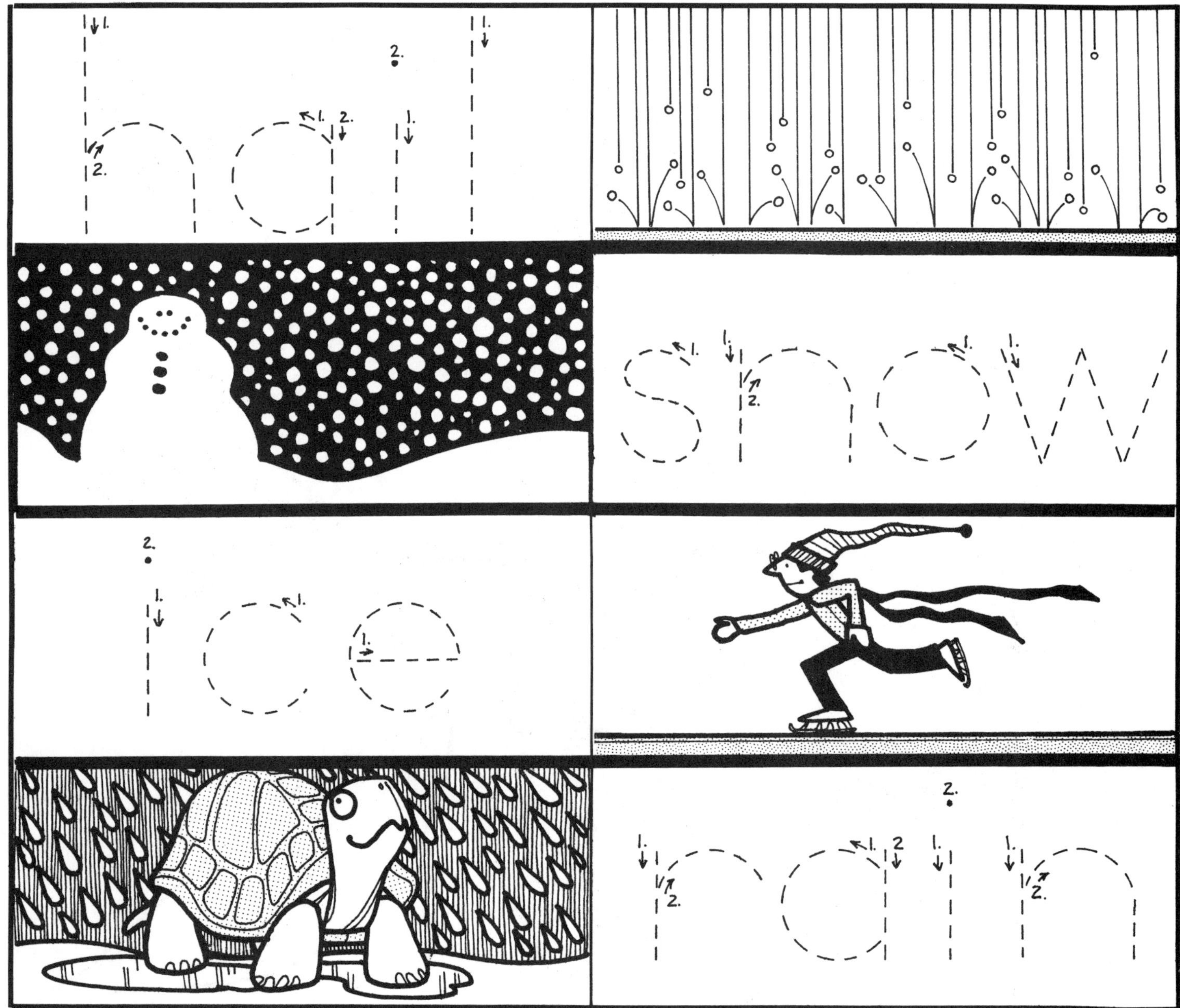

Note to Parents: Beginning to write is like drawing. Children work hard on lines and circles, gradually learning the letters and the sounds for which they stand. Starting at the top of each letter, gently guide your child to do Arrow 1 first. Then go back to Arrow 2 so that the letters are formed correctly. Offer chalk, crayons, or paints for additional letter play. (See page 8, Water in the Weather.)

Skills: Counting
Number Recognition
Fine Motor Skills
Eye-Hand Coordination

Fish Fun

Cut out the circles below. Count the fish in each circle. Look at the numbers written in the boxes. Paste each circle beside the number that tells how many fish are in it.

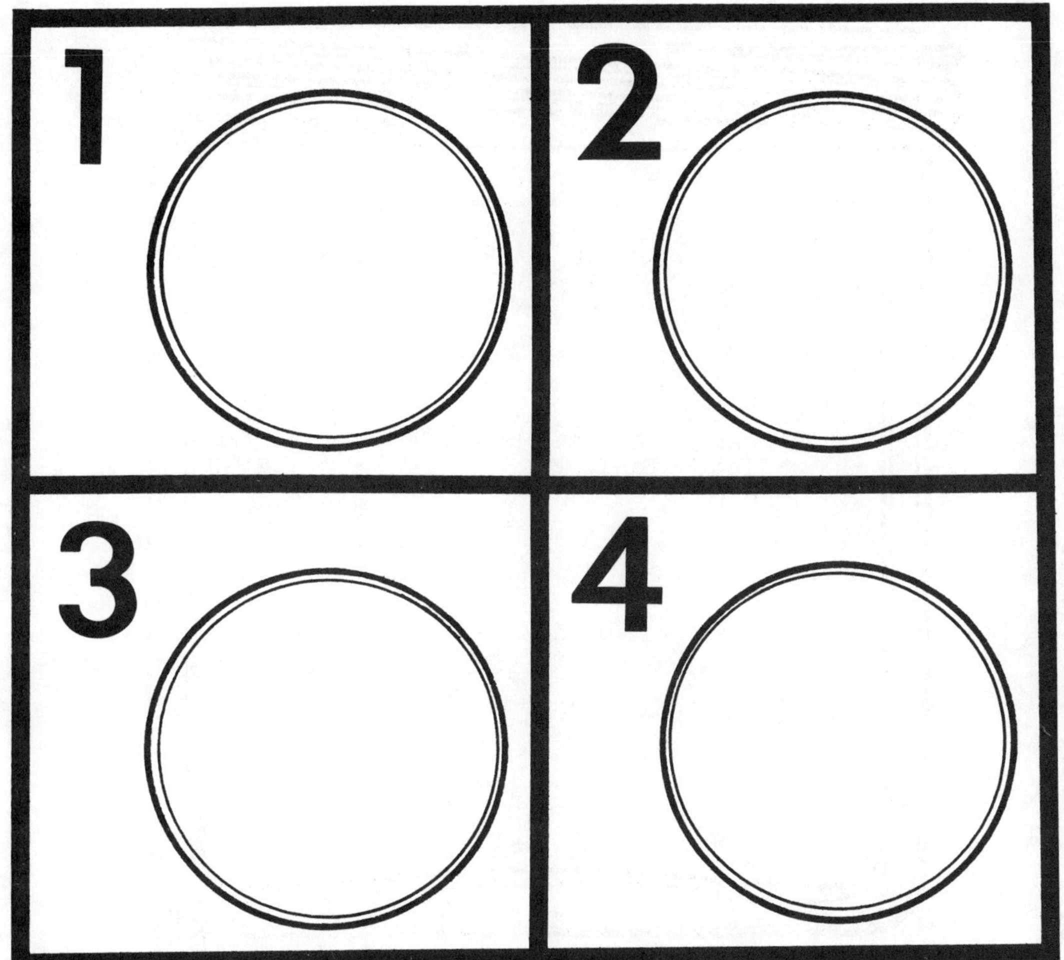

Note to Parents: Provide scissors that really cut, and supervise carefully. Touch-and-say counting helps children begin to understand numbers. With one fish, touch the fish and say, *One.* With two fish, touch the left fish and say, *One.* Then touch the right fish and say, *Two.* For more practice, cut out some brightly colored fish and use touch-and-say counting with your youngster. (See page 7, When Water Is Home.)

Skills: Experimentation
Observation
Associating Ideas

Sink or Float?

When things are dropped in water, some of them sink to the bottom and some of them float on top. Cut out the pictures on this page. Paste the things that **float** at the top of the jar. Paste the things that **sink** at the bottom.

Note to Parents: This page and the page on the back of it are designed to cut and paste. If *sink* and *float* are new ideas for your child, try real objects to find out what happens.

Skills: Making Comparisons
Visual Perception
Seeing Relationships

Find the Water Twin

In each row, color the water animal in the box and the other animal that is *exactly* like it.

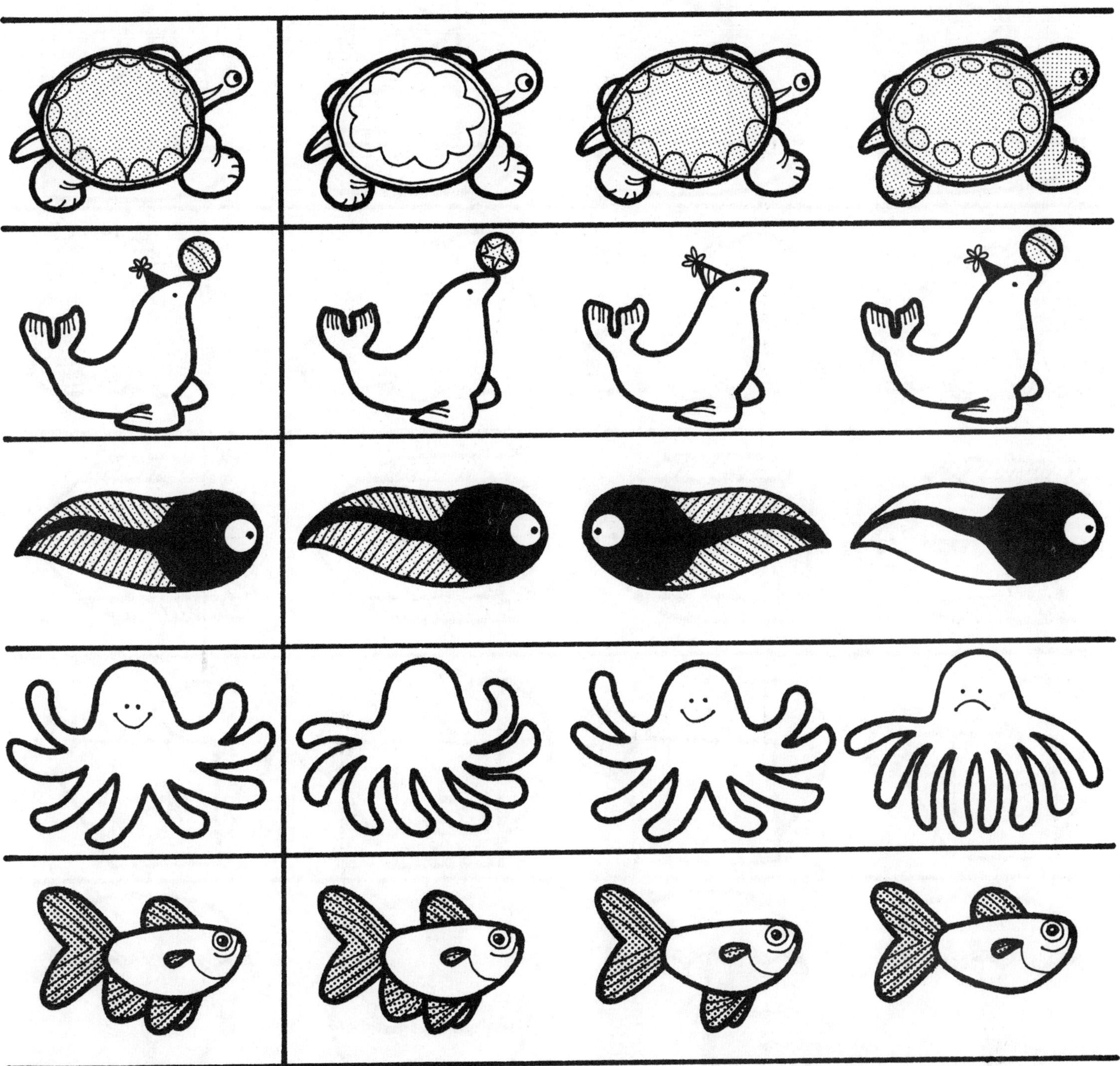

Skills: Making Comparisons
Visual Perception
Seeing Relationships

One Away

In each row, find the one picture that is **different** and color it.

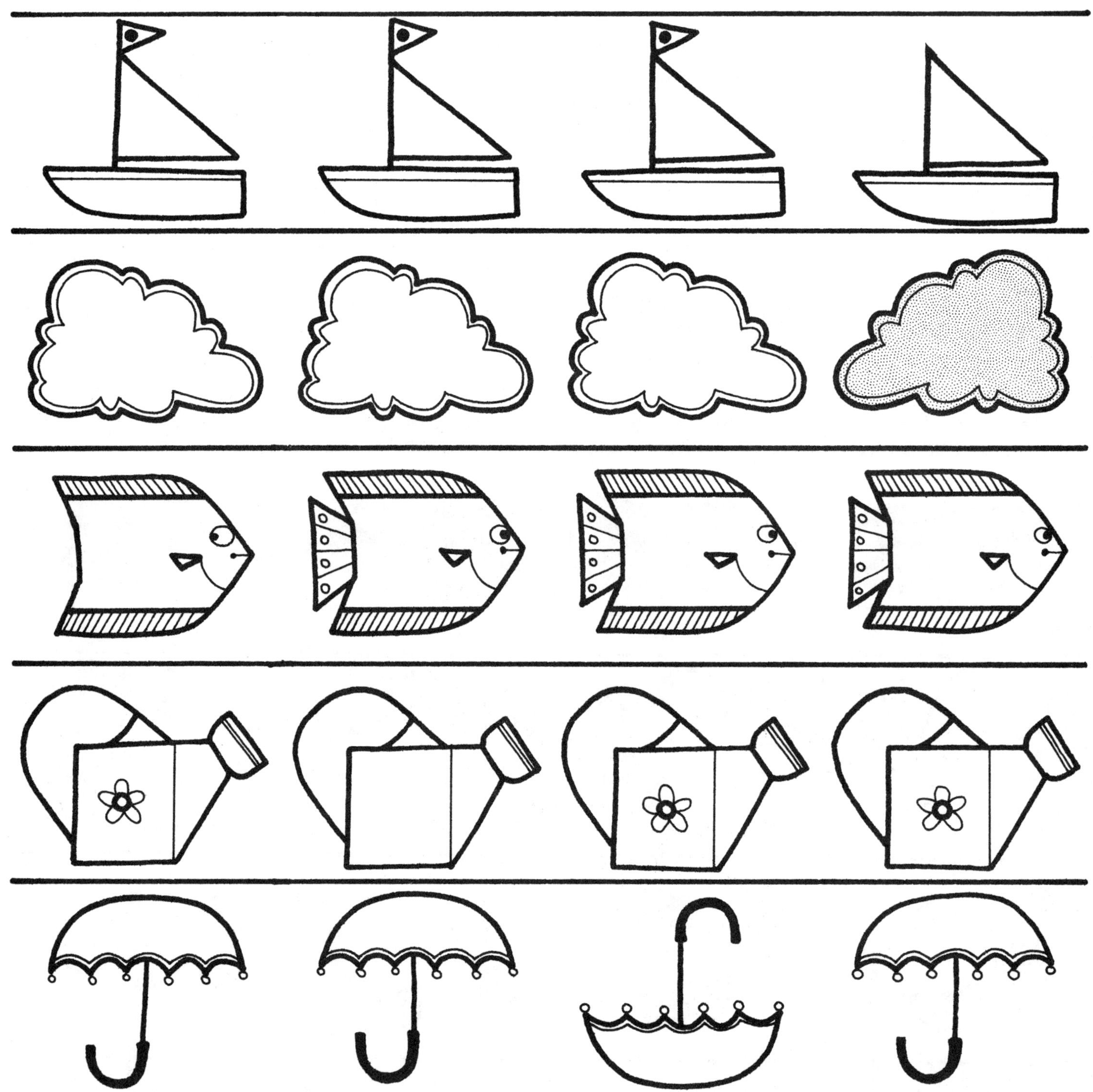

Skills: Ordering
Reasoning
Associating Ideas

Little Boats to Mighty Ships

Color these pictures. Cut them apart. Then sail the boats in order of their size.

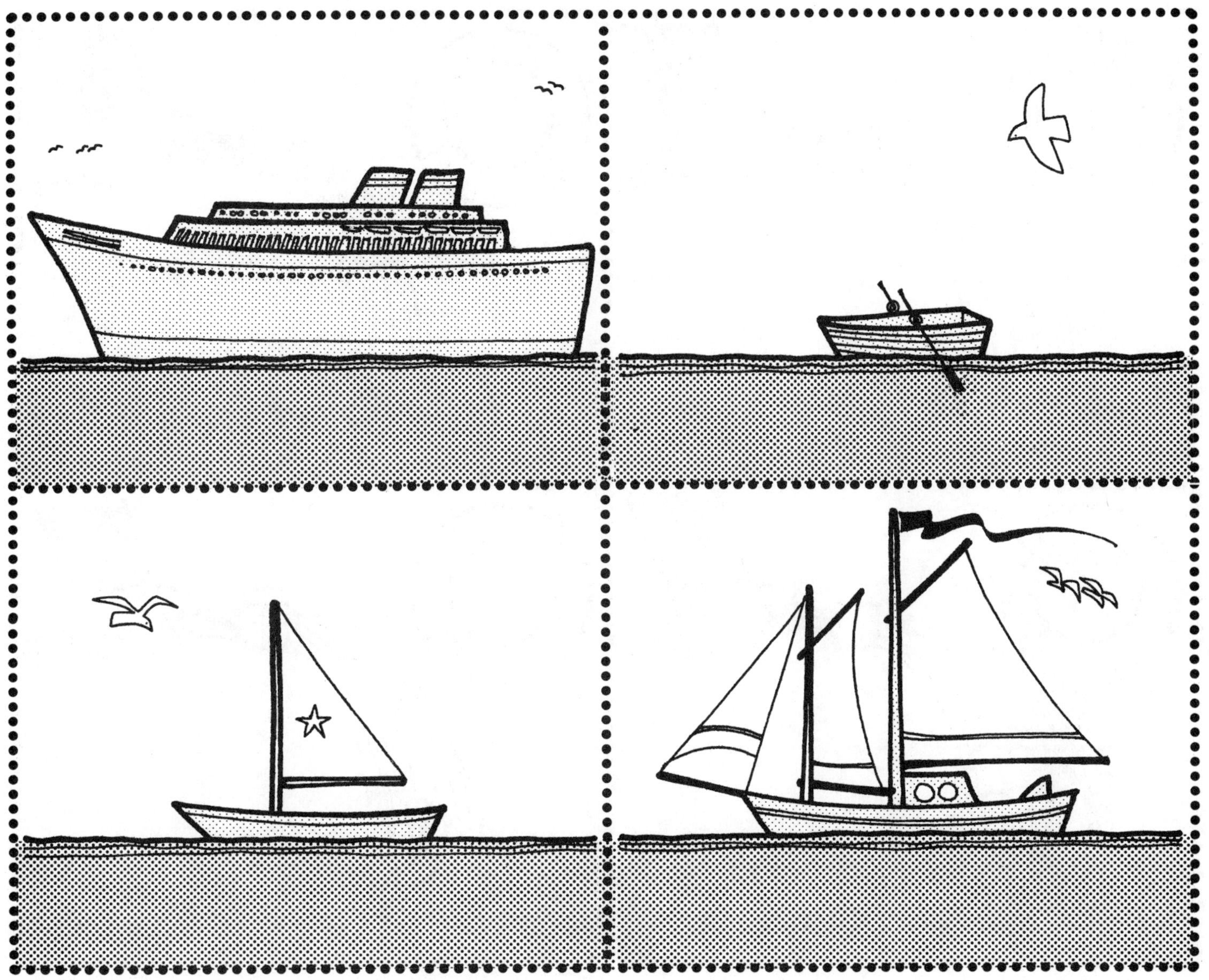

Note to Parents: This page and the one that follows can be cut apart to make games. You could reproduce these pages before cutting to keep the book intact. Let children do the cutting if they are able. Arrange the boats in order from smallest to largest, or largest to smallest. Add other boat pictures to the game. (See page 6, Water All Around.)

Skills: Sequencing
Fine Motor Skills
Visual Perception

Watch Me Grow

How does a plant grow? What happens first? Cut the pictures apart. Then arrange them to show what happens when a plant grows.

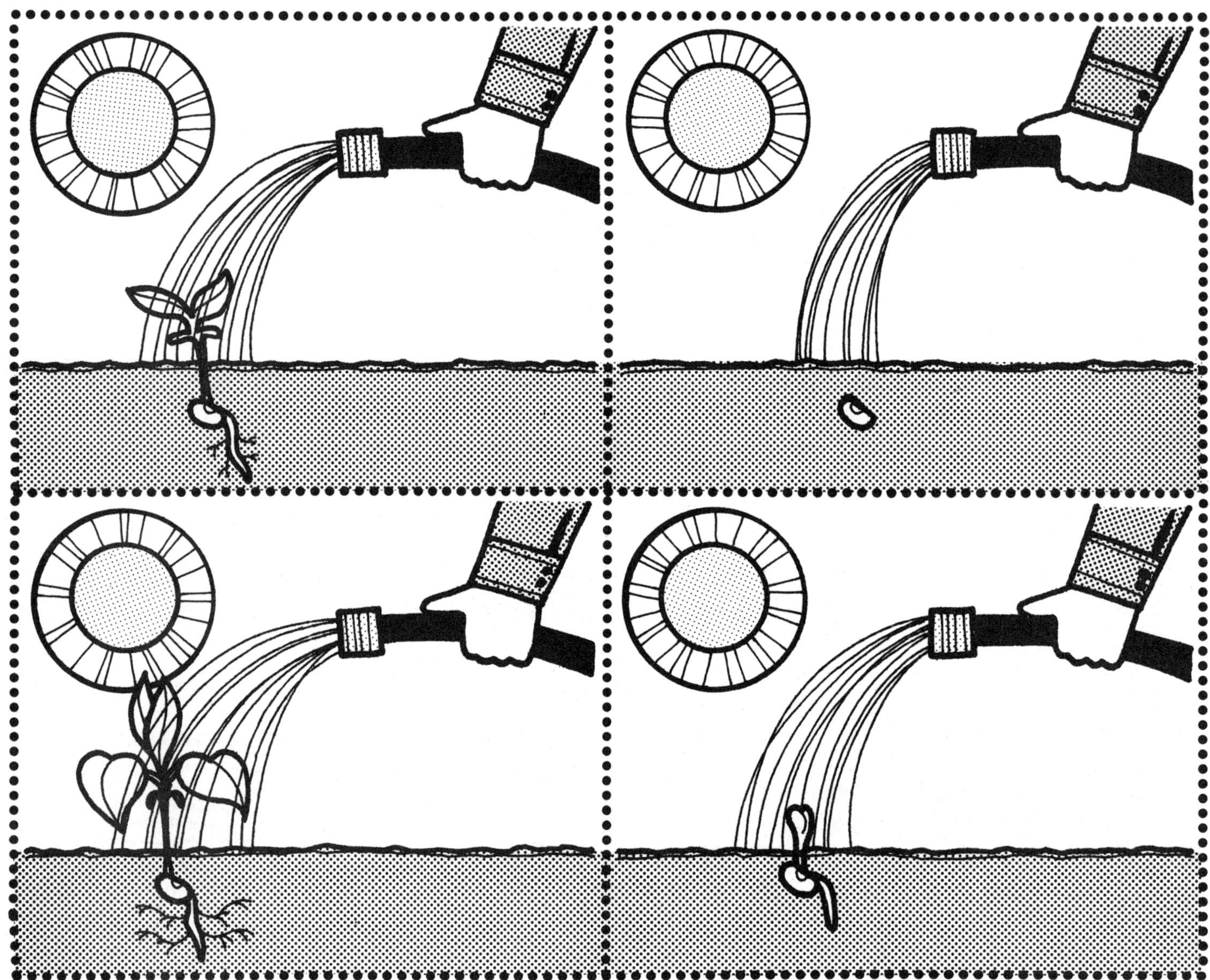

Note to Parents: This page and the one before it can be cut apart to make games. You could reproduce the pages before cutting to keep the book intact. Let children do the cutting if they are able.

Talk about watering plants and crops as one important way we use water. Go through the growing cycle from tiny seed to grown plant. Then help your child review this sequence by putting the pictures in order. Children who are ready can work independently. (See page 5, Water at Work.)